MEZE

MEZE

RENA SALAMAN

photography by Peter Cassidy

RYLAND
PETERS
& SMALL

LONDON NEW YORK

First published in Great Britain in 2006
by Ryland Peters & Small
20–21 Jockey's Fields
London WC1R 4BW
www.rylandpeters.com

10 9 8 7 6 5 4 3 2 1

Printed in China

ISBN-10: 1 84597 135 3
ISBN-13: 978 1 84597 135 9

A CIP record for this book is available
from the British Library.

Senior Designer Steve Painter
Commissioning Editor
  Elsa Petersen-Schepelern
Editor Rachel Lawrence
Production Gavin Bradshaw and
  Gemma Moules
Art Director Anne-Marie Bulat
Editorial Director Julia Charles
Publishing Director Alison Starling

Food Stylist Linda Tubby
Stylist Róisín Nield
Index Hilary Bird

Notes
• All spoon measurements are level,
unless otherwise specified.
• All eggs are medium, unless otherwise
specified. Recipes containing raw or
partially cooked egg, or raw fish or
shellfish, should not be served to the
very young, very old, anyone with a
compromised immune system or
pregnant women.

Dedication
To my lovely daughters, Sophie and
Alexandra.

Author's Acknowledgements
I feel very privileged to have so many
friends who are wonderful cooks. I am
indebted to all of them.

First, my friends in London, Sami
Zubaida and Tatiana Butter who both
made different but delicious kibbeh, and
also to Anissa Helou, Cecile Harris and
Ange de Vena.

I am particularly indebted to my friends
on the Aegean island of Alonnisos who
have taught me so many things over
the years.

My friend Magda Bessini and Katinoula
Agallou for their mouthwatering cheese
pies, courgette fritters and goat yiouvetsi.

All the lovely Alonnisian ladies at the
Women's Co-operative in Patitiri. It is
always such a pleasure to walk into
their shop and be engulfed by delicious
cooking aromas.

My friend Maria Tzezairlithou in Athens
and my sisters Sally Printziou and Maria
Fokianithou.

Finally, my friend Yiota and her husband
Stavros in Volos who own 'To Kanaraki',
one of the best restaurants in Greece.

Of course the book would not have
materialized without the inspiration
and dedication of my lovely editor
Elsa Petersen-Schepelern.

contents

meze culture

Mention the word meze and it instantly evokes celebration and excess. Is it a cultural anomaly or a celebration of the senses? Either way it is embedded in Mediterranean culture, particularly eastern Mediterranean, although we must not forget the gastronomic exuberance of tapas in Spain. When we were children, the Greek words *meze* (singular), *mezethes* (plural) and *mezethaki* (the diminutive form), were magical words. They meant that we would have a celebration and a feast and we loved a good party.

A meze can be a simple appetizer or a complete meal. In Greece, it might be a small plate of olives, a few salted anchovies or small cubes of feta cheese sprinkled with olive oil to accompany an evening ouzo, often referred to as a *mezethaki*.

However, meze evolves and changes to fit the occasion. The more important the occasion or the guests, the more intricate the dishes. At its most elaborate, as with Lebanese meze, it can be a glorious banquet. How could I ever forget the beguiling array of dishes and their aromas in the garden of the Hotel Commodore in Beirut in the spring and summer of 1964 and 1965, when I was an air-stewardess with Olympic Airways? The hoummus, the tabbouleh, the intricate little pastries, the kibbeh, the kebabs! Among the colourful mountains of fruit and vegetables in the labyrinthine central market the paper funnels of golden falafels, the sizzling chicken and the kebabs were addictive. They were followed by cooling fresh fruit juices bought from wandering sellers on the fashionable waterfront, the Corniche.

Whenever our friends on the Aegean island of Alonnisos invite us to dinner, we know that delicious kolokythokeftethes or glistening green dolmathes, bursting with the aromas of the hillsides, will be waiting for us. And these are only the appetizers!

Htipiti means 'beaten' and *tyri* means 'cheese', so *tyrohtipiti* means 'beaten cheese'. It originated in the beautiful city of Thessaloniki, but is fast becoming popular all over Greece. I have had it recently in an *ouzeri* (ouzo and meze restaurant) on the waterfront in Volos. The only difference is its colour, which varies according to the type of peppers used and the heat of the chillies. In Volos, it ranges from pink to red, while in Thessaloniki it is green (see opposite).

feta and chilli dip

HTIPITI OR TYROHTIPITI

2 fresh green chillies

1 large red or green pepper

250 g feta cheese, thickly sliced

4 tablespoons extra virgin olive oil

freshly squeezed juice
of 1 small lemon

3–4 tablespoons milk

1 teaspoon hot red chilli flakes,
such as Greek boukovo

1 tablespoon finely chopped
fresh flat leaf parsley

freshly ground black pepper

toasted bread or crudités,
to serve

a metal skewer

SERVES 6

Thread the chillies on a metal skewer and put over a low gas flame or on a preheated barbecue. Turn them over until scorched. Put the pepper over the flame and do the same until it feels soft and partially scorched. The pepper will take longer than the chillies. Set aside until cool enough to handle.

Deseed and peel the red pepper and do the same with the chillies, which will be a little more difficult. Wipe off any blackened bits with kitchen paper. (Beware of the hot chillies.)

Put the chillies, pepper, feta, olive oil, lemon juice, milk and pepper in a food processor and blend until creamy. If too stiff, add a little more milk. Remove to a plate or bowl, sprinkle the chilli flakes and parsley on top and chill lightly. Serve with toast or crudités.

DIPS AND
SALADS

My introduction to this spicy Middle Eastern chickpea dip was in Beirut in the early '60s when I started flying with Olympic Airways. I was puzzled and thrilled at the same time, as I had never tasted anything like it before. It was served either simply with grilled pita bread or with spicy kebabs or garlicky grilled poussin. It was always present among the exotic array of dishes on meze tables everywhere from Beirut to Byblos.

175 g dried chickpeas, soaked in cold water overnight, or 800 g canned chickpeas

2 tablespoons tahini paste

2 garlic cloves, chopped

freshly squeezed juice of 1–2 lemons

1 tablespoon ground cumin

2 tablespoons extra virgin olive oil

300 ml chickpea cooking liquid

sea salt and freshly ground black pepper

TO SERVE

1 tablespoon extra virgin olive oil

1 tablespoon fresh coriander, finely chopped

pita bread or triangles of toasted bread

SERVES 6

spicy middle eastern chickpea dip

HOUMMUS

Drain and rinse the soaked chickpeas and put them in a saucepan. Cover with plenty of water, bring to the boil and skim until clear. Cover and cook until perfectly soft, about 1 hour. Alternatively, use a pressure cooker, following the manufacturer's instructions – cooking will take about 20 minutes.

Strain the chickpeas, reserving the cooking liquid. If using canned chickpeas, strain them first and discard the liquid, but use about 4 tablespoons cold water in the food processor.

If the tahini paste appears separated in the jar, mix it properly first. Divide all the ingredients into 2 batches and put the first batch in a food processor, then process briefly. Ideally it should still have some texture and should not be too solid. Taste and adjust the seasoning with salt and pepper and blend again briefly. Transfer to a bowl and repeat with the remaining ingredients.

Trickle a little oil over the top and sprinkle with fresh coriander. Serve at room temperature with pita bread or triangles of toasted bread. In the summer, it is better served lightly chilled.

salted cod's roe dip

TARAMOSALATA

200 g smoked, salted cod's roe (tarama)

4 medium slices of stale bread, crusts removed

freshly squeezed juice of 1 large lemon

125 ml extra virgin olive oil

TO SERVE

1 tablespoon finely chopped fresh flat leaf parsley

4–5 black olives

toasted bread or crudités

SERVES 6

If you are using fresh smoked cod's roe, peel the membrane off the surface and discard.

Soak the bread in a bowl of water for 15 minutes, then remove it, squeeze it as dry as you can and put it in a food processor. Add the cod's roe and the lemon juice, process and drizzle in the olive oil to form a smooth creamy paste. Taste and, if it is too sharp and strong, add a little more bread or olive oil according to your taste. Transfer to a plate, cover with clingfilm and chill lightly.

Before serving, sprinkle with the parsley and dot the olives on top. Serve with toasted bread or crudités.

walnut and pepper dip

MUHAMMARA

150 g shelled walnuts

4 medium slices of bread

3 ripe red peppers, deseeded

2 garlic cloves, crushed

grated zest and freshly squeezed juice of 1 unwaxed lemon

2 tablespoons pomegranate syrup

1 green chilli, deseeded

5 tablespoons extra virgin olive oil

a small bunch of parsley, chopped, 3 sprigs reserved

a handful of fresh mint leaves

sea salt

TO SERVE

a handful of pomegranate seeds

pita bread or crudités

SERVES 6

Spread the walnuts over a roasting tin and cook in a preheated oven at 150°C (300°F) Gas 2 for 10 minutes. Toast the bread, then cut off and discard the crusts. Put the bread and cooled walnuts in a food processor and grind to breadcrumb consistency.

Chop the peppers, then add to the food processor. Add the garlic, lemon zest and juice, pomegranate syrup, chilli and salt and process until creamy. With the motor running, add the olive oil and then the fresh herbs at the very end.

Cover with clingfilm and chill lightly. Transfer to a bowl, sprinkle with pomegranate seeds and sprigs of parsley and serve with pita bread or crudités.

The aubergine is one of the most important participants in the meze table. It can be simply grilled over a wood fire outdoors and served in strips with olive oil, lemon and garlic, or pulped into a salad with other ingredients. It is also fried and served with cooling sauces like Tzatziki (page 16), or made into elaborate dishes, such as Imam Bayildi (page 39). Baba Ghanoush is a Middle Eastern classic – rich and utterly seductive.

aubergine purée salad

BABA GHANOUSH

900 g or 3 large aubergines, rinsed and dried

2 tablespoons tahini paste

2 garlic cloves, crushed

freshly squeezed juice of 1 lemon

sea salt and freshly ground black pepper

TO SERVE

1 tablespoon extra virgin olive oil

2 tablespoons finely chopped fresh flat leaf parsley

3 tablespoons pomegranate seeds

SERVES 6

Prick the whole aubergines with a fork to stop them exploding and put them directly on the oven shelves. Roast in a preheated oven at 180°C (350°F) Gas 4 for just under 1 hour, turning them over occasionally.

The trick after this is to remove them from the oven and lay them directly on a gentle gas flame for 2–3 minutes. Using oven gloves, hold them by their stalks and keep turning them over as they are scorched. This is quite a tricky business, but it will give you that inimitable smoky taste.

Remove from the heat, let cool enough to handle, slit them open and spoon the flesh into a colander to drain. Press lightly to extract the juices. Put in a food processor with the remaining ingredients and pulse briefly to form a coarse paste. Taste and add salt and pepper as necessary.

Spread on a platter, drizzle the olive oil in a decorative pattern, sprinkle the parsley and pomegranate seeds on top and serve.

Note The best way to cook aubergines is always over charcoal so they are infused with a smoky aroma. However, this is not always practical so in this recipe I have improvised a little to get the desired effect.

cucumber yoghurt dip

TZATZIKI

200 g plain Greek yoghurt

12 cm piece of cucumber, peeled and thickly grated

1 garlic clove, crushed

1 tablespoon extra virgin olive oil

½ teaspoon red wine vinegar

1 tablespoon finely chopped fresh mint

sea salt

SERVES 6

This refreshing dip is an ideal partner for barbecued meats or vegetables, or Tyropitta Alonnisou (page 31).

Put the yoghurt in a bowl and add the cucumber. Add the garlic, olive oil, vinegar, mint and salt. Mix well with a fork. Cover with clingfilm and chill lightly.

Note Delicious accompaniments for tzatziki include grilled or fried vegetables. Thinly slice 2 courgettes lengthways and 2 aubergines crossways. Pour 3 cm depth of sunflower or groundnut oil into a frying pan and heat until a haze forms. Working in batches, dredge the sliced vegetables in plain flour, then fry in the hot oil on both sides. Remove and drain on kitchen paper.

lebanese tahini dip

TARATOR

5 tablespoons tahini paste

1 teaspoon ground cumin

100 ml warm water

2 garlic cloves, crushed

freshly squeezed juice of 1½ lemons

3 tablespoons finely chopped fresh flat leaf parsley

sea salt

SERVES 6

In the Lebanon, Tarator is as ubiquitous as tzatziki is in Greece. It is traditionally served with fish or thinned down and used as a salad dressing.

If the tahini paste has separated in the jar, mix it properly with a spoon. Put the tahini in a food processor, add the cumin, water, garlic, salt and half the lemon juice and process until smooth and amalgamated – it should have the consistency of thick cream.

Taste and adjust by adding as much lemon juice as you like. I love sharp lemony tastes, but it is a matter of personal preference.

Transfer to a bowl, stir in the parsley and serve.

Summers in Greece would not be complete without *horiatiki salata*, which can be a meal in itself. *Horiatiki* means 'peasant or country salad' and it is derived from the word *horio* – 'village'. It is delicious made with ripe sugary tomatoes and a generous amount of an aromatic olive oil, such as Mani or Karyatis from Peloponnisos. It is even better eaten under a magnificent olive tree beside a dazzling beach and makes a perfect partner for many dishes, particularly grilled kebabs and fried vegetables or cheese pies.

400 g ripe sweet tomatoes

1 small red onion, thinly sliced

1 green pepper, deseeded and sliced into thin ribbons

10 cm piece of cucumber, thinly sliced

150 g feta cheese, crumbled

6 8 black or green olives

5–6 tablespoons extra virgin olive oil

a large pinch of dried oregano

sea salt and freshly ground black pepper

SERVES 6

tomato, cucumber, onion and feta salad

HORIATIKI SALATA

Cut the tomatoes in quarters lengthways and cut out the stalk pieces. Cut the quarters into bite-sized wedges and put in a bowl.

Add the onion, green pepper, cucumber, feta cheese, olives, olive oil, oregano, salt and pepper and toss to coat with the olive oil and infuse with the oregano. Keep at room temperature for at least 30 minutes before serving.

Tabbouleh is the crown of Lebanese meze. I still remember the starlit night in the early '60s when I tasted it for the first time in the garden of the Hotel Commodore in central Beirut. It gave me a veritable sense of *The Thousand and One Nights*. I must admit that the jasmine-scented air in the garden mingling with the grilling kebab smells must have helped. Tabbouleh is predominantly a green herby salad full of aromas, so the proportion of wheat to herbs is vital. Ideally herbs should always be chopped by hand rather than mashed up in a food processor. This is particularly true of this dish, so I always use my husband instead.

lebanese parsley salad
TABBOULEH

85 g coarse bulghur (cracked wheat), picked clean of stones

200 g bunch of flat leaf parsley, trimmed of thick stalks

a small bunch of mint, leaves chopped

10 cm piece of cucumber, peeled and diced

1 red onion or 4 spring onions, finely chopped

2 tomatoes, about 250 g, peeled and diced

½ green pepper, deseeded and diced

VINAIGRETTE

freshly squeezed juice of 1–2 lemons

4–5 tablespoons extra virgin olive oil

a large pinch of ground allspice

sea salt and freshly ground black pepper

lettuce leaves or vine leaves, to serve (optional)

SERVES 6

Put the bulghur in a fine sieve and rinse it under cold running water. Put in a bowl and soak in warm water for 20 minutes. Drain and pat dry in a clean tea towel to get rid of excess moisture. Transfer to a large bowl.

Coarsely chop the parsley and add to the bowl. Add the mint, cucumber, onion, tomatoes and pepper, then mix well. Cover with clingfilm and chill lightly.

Just before serving, put the juice of 1 lemon in a bowl, add the olive oil, allspice, salt and pepper and beat lightly. Pour over the salad and toss to coat well.

Taste and adjust the seasoning, adding more lemon juice, if needed. It should have a refreshing tangy taste. Line a platter or bowl with the lettuce or vine leaves and heap the salad on top.

This is the winter salad *par excellence* in Greece. Come October and you find its refreshing taste everywhere on the Greek table. Greek women pride themselves on how thinly they slice the cabbage. It was my sister's idea to add the cheese, and my own to add the pomegranate seeds – hard to resist.

cabbage salad with pomegranate

LAHANOSALATA ME ROTHI

1 white cabbage

1 pomegranate

2 carrots, scraped and grated

2–3 tablespoons finely chopped fresh flat leaf parsley

100 g Greek feta cheese, cut into cubes

6–8 green or black olives

VINAIGRETTE

6 tablespoons extra virgin olive oil

freshly squeezed juice of 1 lemon

1 garlic clove, crushed

sea salt

SERVES 6

Remove and discard the outer leaves and the hard stem of the cabbage. Cut the head into quarters and trim off any obvious hard bits.

Put each quarter on its side and cut long, very thin slices until you reach the central core, which should be discarded.

Cut the pomegranate in quarters, then patiently extract the jewel-like scarlet seeds by hand over a plate to catch all the delicious juices. (Believe me it is worth the effort.)

Put the cabbage in a bowl with the carrots, parsley, feta, olives, pomegranate seeds and juices and toss well.

To make the vinaigrette, put the olive oil, lemon juice, garlic and salt in a bowl and beat well. Pour over the salad, toss until everything is thoroughly coated, then serve.

Saganaki takes its name from the small double-handled frying pan in which it is usually served sizzling, either in tavernas or at home. Traditionally, Greek Kefalotyri cheese, which is quite salty and full of flavour, is used for this meze dish. Cypriot Haloumi also makes an appetizing alternative. If these aren't available, however, you can basically fry any strong-tasting cheese that will not melt in the process.

fried cheese

SAGANAKI

12 slices of Kefalotyri, Kasseri or Haloumi, about 1 cm thick

3 tablespoons plain flour

3–4 tablespoons light olive or groundnut oil

TO SERVE

1 tablespoon finely chopped fresh flat leaf parsley

2 lemons, quartered

freshly ground black pepper

SERVES 6

Coat each slice of cheese lightly in flour and shake any excess. Heat half the olive oil in a non-stick frying pan and put half the slices in a single layer. Leave them for a couple of minutes and then turn them over as their edges get crisp and golden. Let them lightly brown on the other side, about 1 minute, then place them on a double layer of kitchen paper in order to get rid of excess oil.

Heat a little more oil in the frying pan and, when hot, repeat as before with the remaining cheese.

Serve immediately on a platter with a little black pepper and the parsley sprinkled all over, and surrounded by lemon wedges.

CHEESE AND
SAVOURY PASTRIES

Sambusak are intricate little pastries with sweet and sour flavours and delicious aromas. Traditionally fried, they can also be baked.

spicy meat pastries

SAMBUSAK

175 g plain flour

½ teaspoon sea salt

2 tablespoons olive oil

90 ml water

1 egg yolk, lightly beaten

FILLING

3–4 tablespoons olive oil

1 large onion, finely chopped

200 g lean minced lamb

1 teaspoon ground allspice

1 teaspoon ground cumin

a large pinch of ground cinnamon

freshly squeezed juice of 1 lemon

3 tablespoons raisins, rinsed

150 ml hot water

3 tablespoons finely chopped fresh mint leaves

2 tablespoons pine nuts, toasted in a dry frying pan

sea salt and freshly ground black pepper

a round 8 cm pastry cutter

an oiled baking sheet

MAKES ABOUT 30

To make the pastry, sift the flour and salt into a bowl. Make a well in the centre, add the oil and mix with your fingers. Add the water and knead until a soft, neat ball is formed. Cover with clingfilm and let rest for 30 minutes.

Heat the oil in a saucepan, add the onion and sauté until it turns light brown, about 10 minutes. Increase the heat and add the minced lamb, turning and breaking up the lumps until all the moisture has evaporated and it starts to sizzle. Add the allspice, cumin, cinnamon, salt and pepper and brown for 2–3 minutes. Add the lemon juice, raisins and the hot water, cover and cook for 20 minutes. It should be a fairly dry mixture by then. Add the mint and pine nuts and set aside.

Divide the pastry in half. Put one piece on a lightly floured surface and roll out thinly to a circle about 30 cm diameter, turning the pastry frequently. Cut out rounds with the pastry cutter. Gather the remaining pastry from around the discs and add it to the remaining portion of pastry. Knead until soft again, cover and set aside.

Have a small bowl of cold water by you. Put 1 teaspoon of filling in the middle of a round of pastry. Dip a finger in the water and wet the edges, then fold half of the pastry over the other half making a half-moon shape. Press the edges firmly to seal and put it on the baking sheet. Repeat until all the rounds have been used. Roll out the remaining pastry, cut out more rounds and repeat the process.

Brush the tops with the egg yolk and bake in a preheated oven at 200°C (400°F) Gas 6 for 10–12 minutes until light golden.

Pastries are at the heart of Greek food and culture and each village and every island has its own indigenous versions that act like a showcase to local produce. This sensational pie is the most common and most delicious.

spinach and cheese pie
SPANAKOTYROPITTA

1 packet filo pastry, 400 g, thawed if frozen

150 g butter, melted

FILLING

500 g fresh leaf spinach, rinsed

4 tablespoons extra virgin olive oil

1 large onion, finely chopped

4–5 spring onions, trimmed and coarsely chopped

4 eggs

250 g feta cheese

90 g fresh dill, finely chopped

3–4 tablespoons finely chopped fresh flat leaf parsley

4 tablespoons milk

sea salt and freshly ground black pepper

a roasting tin, about 35 x 30 cm

MAKES ABOUT 12 PIECES

To make the filling, put the spinach in a large saucepan of water, cover and cook gently, stirring occasionally, for 5–6 minutes until wilted. Drain the spinach thoroughly in a colander. Wipe the saucepan dry, add the olive oil and sauté the onion and spring onions until translucent. Add the spinach, salt and pepper and sauté for 4–5 minutes. Let cool a little. Beat the eggs in a large bowl, crumble in the cheese, add the herbs, milk and spinach and mix well with a fork.

Unroll the pastry carefully – you will have an oblong stack of paper-thin sheets. Brush the roasting tin with the hot melted butter. Then butter sparingly the top sheet of pastry and lay it into the tin, folding any excess on one side (keep in mind that the pastry will shrink when cooked). Continue the same way folding the excess on alternate ends until you have used about half the pastry. Add the filling and spread it evenly. Fold the sides over it and start covering with the remaining pastry sheets, brushing each one with the melted butter. Try to be as neat as possible.

Finally, brush the top layer of pastry generously with butter. Using a sharp knife, score the top layers of pastry into diamond or square shapes – do it carefully to avoid spilling the filling. Using your fingertips, sprinkle a little cold water on top to stop the pastry curling.

Bake in a preheated oven at 190°C (375°F) Gas 5 for 50 minutes until golden on top. (It is nice to have it still a little moist in the centre.) Slice carefully all the way to the bottom sheets of pastry and serve hot or at room temperature.

These delicious cheese pies are part of the local tradition on the island of Alonnisos. There is a hidden granny in every restaurant's kitchen making them. It is the first thing little girls learn to make and they do it with astounding results. It is sensational eaten straight out of the frying pan. In the summer, we can order them from the Women's Co-operative, then pick them up hot and crisp for a perfect lunch at home by the sea.

traditional cheese pie

TYROPITTA ALONNISOU

250 g plain flour

a pinch of sea salt

2 teaspoons olive oil, plus 6–7 tablespoons for frying

150 ml cold water

220 g feta cheese

2 tablespoons extra virgin olive oil

MAKES 2 PIES: SERVES 6–12

Sift the flour and salt into a bowl, add the 2 teaspoons olive oil and the water and mix until it becomes an elastic, neat ball. Transfer to a floured work surface and start stretching and kneading with the palm of your hand for 5 minutes. Cover with clingfilm and let rest for at least 30 minutes.

Divide the dough in two and roll out the pieces, one at a time, on a floured surface into a large circle, preferably using a thin rolling pin. Keep turning the dough round and over, sprinkling a little flour, until you have a thin pastry circle of about 60 cm diameter.

Crumble half the cheese all over the circle, sprinkle with 1 tablespoon olive oil and start folding the pie. First roll the two diametrically opposite sides like two fat cigars until they meet at the centre. Now comes the clever bit – holding one end of the pastry down, roll the opposite end round it like a flat snail.

Heat the oil over medium heat in a large frying pan, lift the cheese pie with a flat spatula and slide it into the pan. Fry until light golden on the underside, then turn it over carefully and fry it on the other side. The whole frying operation is swift and it takes about 6–7 minutes. Remove and put on a plate lined with kitchen paper. Repeat with the remaining pastry and serve immediately.

Gigandes, which means 'giants' in Greek, resemble butter beans, but are fuller and much sweeter. They are piled high in white glistening mounds in the stalls of the *laiki* (street markets) where they are sometimes also called *elephandes* (elephants). The most delicious gigandes come from Kastoria in the north of Greece. They can be found in Greek grocers and Italian or Spanish delicatessens. Gigandes always appear on restaurant menus throughout the year.

400 g dried Greek fasolia gigandes or butter beans, soaked overnight in cold water to cover

150 ml extra virgin olive oil

2 large onions, about 500 g, chopped

3 garlic cloves, thinly sliced

1 red pepper, deseeded and diced

1 celery stalk, trimmed, rinsed and sliced

2 carrots, thinly sliced

1 teaspoon dried oregano

1 teaspoon dried thyme

400 g canned tomatoes, chopped

2 tablespoons tomato purée, diluted with 450 ml hot water

½ teaspoon sugar

4 tablespoons finely chopped fresh flat leaf parsley

sea salt and freshly ground black pepper

SERVES 6

giant beans baked with garlic and tomatoes

GIGANDES

Rinse the beans, put them in a saucepan with plenty of cold water, cover and boil until they are almost cooked. Keep an eye on them as they cook quickly, about 30 minutes. They should not be allowed to disintegrate. Drain and discard the water.

Heat the olive oil in the saucepan, add the onions and sauté until light golden. Add the garlic and fry for 2 minutes. Add the pepper, celery, carrots, oregano and thyme and sauté for 5–6 minutes.

Add the tomatoes, diluted tomato purée and sugar, cover and cook for 10 minutes. Add the beans, season with salt and pepper and cook gently for a further 15 minutes.

Stir in the parsley, transfer to a large ovenproof dish and cook in preheated oven at 180°C (350°F) Gas 4 for 30 minutes, or until browned around the edges. Serve hot or at room temperature. This is an ideal dish to make in advance.

BEANS AND VEGETABLES

I discovered falafels – like so many other things – in the early '60s on trips to Cairo and Beirut. I remember buying a paper funnel filled with freshly fried falafels in the central vegetable market in Beirut. They were totally addictive. Even my grandmother in Athens became a devotee and I used to bring sizeable quantities back for her from my overnight stopovers in those Middle Eastern cities. Falafels are very good served with Hoummus (page 11), Tarator (page 16) or Tzatziki (page 16), and a refreshing salad like Lahanosalata Me Rothi (page 23).

spicy broad bean patties
FALAFEL

250 g dried, skinless broad beans, soaked overnight in cold water to cover

1 large onion, about 400 g, coarsely chopped

2 garlic cloves, crushed

1 tablespoon ground cumin

1 tablespoon ground coriander

1 teaspoon ground allspice

¼ teaspoon cayenne pepper

¼ teaspoon baking powder

200 g bunch of fresh parsley

a handful of fresh coriander

groundnut or sunflower oil, for deep-frying

MAKES ABOUT 20

Drain and rinse the beans. Put them in a food processor, then add the onion, garlic, cumin, ground coriander, allspice, cayenne pepper and baking powder. Process to an almost-smooth paste – I like it to be a little grainy.

Add the parsley and coriander and process briefly again. The greenery should be coarsely chopped and identifiable. (You may have to divide the ingredients in half and process in 2 batches, depending on the size of your processor). Empty into a bowl and set aside for at least 1 hour.

Take 1 tablespoon of the mixture and shape it between your palms into a flat round shape, about 5–6 cm diameter. Continue until all the mixture has been used.

Just before serving, heat 1 cm depth of oil in a large non-stick frying pan, add a single layer of the falafels and fry until golden and crisp on one side, then turning them over to crisp on the other side. Remove with a slotted spoon and drain on a plate lined with kitchen paper. Repeat until all the falafels have been fried. They are delicious served hot or at room temperature.

Fava is always part of meze in Greece. Although quite frugal, it is one of the first plates to arrive on the table, even at glittering restaurants such as Vlassis in Athens. (If you want to experience meze at its most glorious, go to Vlassis – it has the most dazzling array.) This dish has been on the Greek menu for several thousand years. Etnos, popular in classical Athens according to Aristophanes, is almost identical, so this is a Greek classic in every sense! Authentic Greek fava (the best come from the island of Santorini) may look similar to yellow split peas, but they have a much sweeter taste.

yellow split pea purée

FAVA

300 g Greek fava or yellow split peas

2 onions, finely chopped

2 tablespoons capers, rinsed

5–6 tablespoons extra virgin olive oil

freshly squeezed juice of 1 lemon

4–6 black olives

sea salt and freshly ground black pepper

SERVES 6

Soak the fava or split peas in cold water for 1–2 hours. Drain, rinse, put in a saucepan and cover with 2 litres water. Bring to the boil and skim until clear.

Add just over half the chopped onion and simmer, uncovered, for at least 1 hour, or until perfectly soft. Stir occasionally and add some hot water if needed. At the end of cooking, when the dish has the consistency of thick soup, add salt.

Transfer to a food processor or blender while it is still hot, process until smooth, then pour onto a large platter immediately as it solidifies when cold.

Sprinkle the capers, black pepper and the remaining onion over the top, sprinkle with the olive oil and lemon juice and pile the olives in the middle. Serve warm or at room temperature.

This is a dish full of summer flavours and perfect for meze as it tastes even better served at room temperature. It derives its Turkish name from an old fable about the Turkish priest – the Imam – who fainted either from overindulging in this rich dish or from meanness because of the extravagant amount of the olive oil used.

150 ml extra virgin olive oil

800 g or 3 medium aubergines, rinsed and halved lengthways

sea salt and freshly ground black pepper

STUFFING

2 onions, finely chopped

4 garlic cloves, finely chopped

1 teaspoon ground cumin

500 g ripe tomatoes, chopped

1 tablespoon dried oregano

½ teaspoon sugar

150 ml water

3 tablespoons chopped fresh flat leaf parsley

1 tablespoon tomato purée, diluted with 150 ml hot water

sea salt and freshly ground black pepper

SERVES 6

baked aubergines with garlic and tomatoes

IMAM BAYILDI

Heat half the olive oil in a large frying pan, add 3 pieces of aubergine and shallow-fry, turning them over until light golden on both sides, 10–15 minutes. Remove and rest on kitchen paper. Repeat with the remaining 3 pieces. Arrange the pieces side by side in an ovenproof dish and season with salt and pepper.

To make the stuffing, heat the remaining olive oil in a saucepan, add the onions and sauté gently until they start to colour. Add the garlic and cumin, fry for 2–3 minutes, then add the tomatoes, oregano, salt, pepper, sugar and the water. Cover and cook for 15 minutes, stirring occasionally.

Stir in the parsley, then divide the stuffing into 6 equal portions. Pile each portion along the length of each aubergine half. Add the diluted tomato purée to the dish and cook in a preheated oven 190°C (375°F) Gas 5 for 45 minutes, basting the aubergines once during cooking. Serve hot or at room temperature.

Sharply appetizing, these fritters are cooked in homes and restaurants on our favourite Greek island, Alonnisos. Though a little time-consuming to make, everyone demands them in midsummer, when there is a glut of home-grown deliciously sweet courgettes. Serve with Horiatiki Salata (page 19) or a tomato and rocket salad.

courgette fritters
KOLOKYTHOKEFTETHES ALONNISOU

3 tablespoons extra virgin olive oil

1 large onion, finely chopped

4 spring onions, including green parts, trimmed and chopped

2 garlic cloves, crushed

600 g courgettes, trimmed and rinsed

4 medium slices of bread (not a pre-sliced loaf), toasted and crusts removed

2 small eggs

4 tablespoons self-raising flour, plus 5–6 tablespoons, for rolling

200 g feta cheese, crumbled

100 g grated Parmesan, Gruyère or Cheddar cheese

1 tablespoon dried oregano, such as Greek rigani

3 tablespoons fresh mint, chopped, or 1 tablespoon dried mint

5–6 tablespoons olive oil, for frying

freshly ground black pepper

MAKES ABOUT 15

Heat the olive oil in a frying pan, add the onion and spring onions and sauté gently until translucent, up to 20 minutes. Add the garlic, fry for 1 minute and remove from the heat. Let cool a little.

Grate the courgettes coarsely, put in a colander and set aside for about 30 minutes to let them expel their moisture.

Put the toasted bread in a food processor and process to make breadcrumbs. Put the eggs in a bowl and beat lightly. Squeeze the courgettes with your hands to extract as much moisture as possible – this is very important. Add to the bowl, then add the onion mixture, the 3 tablespoons flour, feta, Parmesan, oregano, mint and pepper. Mix with a fork. It should be dry enough to handle but, if not, add a little more flour.

Put a double sheet of greaseproof paper on a work surface and add the remaining flour. Take 1 tablespoon of the mixture, roll it in the flour, then make a round flat shape with your hands, about 5 cm diameter. The rounds are easier to handle when well coated in flour. Continue until the mixture is finished.

Just before serving, heat the olive oil in a large non-stick frying pan and fry them for about 3 minutes on each side until crisp and golden. Drain on kitchen paper.

With its lush intriguing taste, okra is the beloved vegetable of the Eastern Mediterranean, cooked with or without meat. It is surrounded by an impenetrable mystique but once it has been sampled it becomes an instant success with its fresh taste. I love this vegetarian okra dish because it can be cooked well in advance and will wait happily at a meze table. The dried limes, which can be obtained from Arab or Indian stores, add an altogether new dimension to its sweet taste.

okra with dried limes

BAMYA

800 g fresh okra

150 ml extra virgin olive oil

1 large onion, sliced

1 teaspoon ground coriander

½ teaspoon ground allspice

700 g fresh tomatoes, sliced, or 400 g canned tomatoes

2 dried limes (optional)

½ teaspoon sugar

2 tablespoons finely chopped fresh coriander

sea salt and freshly ground black pepper

SERVES 6

To prepare the okra, pare the conical tops with a sharp knife (similar to peeling potatoes). Put in a bowl, cover with cold water briefly, then drain – handle with care.

Heat the oil in a wide saucepan, add the onion and sauté until light golden. Add the ground coriander and allspice, then when aromatic, add the tomatoes, dried limes, if using, sugar, salt and pepper. Cook for 10 minutes, pressing the limes with a spatula to extract their sour juices.

Add the okra and spread them evenly in the pan. Add enough hot water until they are almost immersed in the sauce.

Cook gently for about 30 minutes – shake the pan occasionally but don't stir as okra is fragile. Sprinkle the fresh coriander over the top and simmer for 5–10 minutes more. Serve warm or at room temperature.

Dolmathes, when made with fresh, young vine leaves in spring, make the most mouthwatering dish in the world for me. There are many versions – they can also be made with a meat stuffing, but this purist's vegetarian version is undoubtedly the star of the show. An exquisite aromatic olive oil, such as Mani from Peloponnisos, is a must. They are time consuming, but invite your friends around and enlist some help.

stuffed vine leaves

DOLMATHES

55 fresh vine leaves, plus extra to serve (optional), or 225 g preserved vine leaves

4 tablespoons extra virgin olive oil

450 ml hot water

STUFFING

freshly squeezed juice of 1 lemon, strained

150 g long grain rice, rinsed

2 large onions, finely chopped (not grated)

5 spring onions, including white parts, trimmed and thinly sliced

4 tablespoons fresh dill, finely chopped

2 tablespoons fresh mint, finely chopped

2 tablespoons finely chopped fresh flat leaf parsley

5 tablespoons extra virgin olive oil

sea salt and freshly ground black pepper

MAKES 50

Bring a large saucepan of water to the boil and blanch the fresh vine leaves for 1–2 minutes in batches of 5–6 at a time. Remove with a slotted spoon and drain in a colander. They should just be wilted. If using preserved leaves, remember they are very salty – rinse first, then soak in a bowl of hot water for 3–5 minutes. Remove, rinse again and drain in a colander.

To make the stuffing, put half the lemon juice in a large bowl. Add the rice, onions, spring onions, dill, mint, parsley, olive oil, salt and pepper and stir well.

Line the base of a wide saucepan with 4 or 5 vine leaves. Place a vine leaf, rough side up, on a chopping board (handle the leaves carefully as they are fragile). Put a heaped teaspoon of the stuffing near the stalk end, fold the 2 opposite sides over the stuffing and roll up tightly like a fat cigar. Repeat with the remaining leaves.

Arrange the stuffed vine leaves in tight circles in the saucepan with the loose ends underneath. Pour the olive oil and the remaining lemon juice over the top and set a small inverted plate on top to stop them opening up while cooking. Add the hot water, cover and simmer gently for 50 minutes.

Serve hot or at room temperature on a platter lined with fresh vine leaves, if available.

For me, there is an aura of golden childhood memories about this dish – we always ate it on sunny Sundays by the sea in Mikrolimano, in the port of Pireas where we lived. A *yiouvetsi* is a traditional glazed, round, dark red earthenware baking dish with no lid, and has given its name to various recipes in Greece. A *yiouvetsaki* is a smaller version of the same dish.

baked prawns with tomatoes and feta cheese

GARITHES YIOUVETSAKI

4 tablespoons extra virgin olive oil

1 onion, finely chopped

1 red pepper, deseeded and chopped

500 g ripe tomatoes, blanched, peeled and coarsely chopped

a large pinch of sugar

½ teaspoon dried oregano, such as Greek rigani

500 g peeled raw tiger or king prawns

3 tablespoons finely chopped fresh flat leaf parsley

125 g Greek feta cheese, cut into cubes

sea salt and freshly ground black pepper

SERVES 6

Heat the olive oil in a frying pan, add the onion and sauté gently until translucent. Add the pepper and cook for 2–3 more minutes.

Add the tomatoes, sugar, oregano, salt and pepper and cook gently for 10–15 minutes until the sauce has thickened.

Add the prawns, parsley and half the cheese, then transfer to a small ovenproof dish and sprinkle the remaining cheese cubes on top. Bake in a preheated oven at 180°C (350°F) Gas 4 for 30 minutes. Serve hot or at room temperature.

This Lenten recipe will be found everywhere in the weeks preceding Greek Orthodox Easter, particularly in island communities. There are also squid risottos, squid with pasta, squid with potatoes and stuffed squid – all ingenious ways to make lovely meals from the plethora of fresh squid so popular in Greece. The bonus is that it tastes even better at room temperature, so is an ideal candidate for mezethes. Taramosalata (page 12) or Fava (page 36) make excellent partners.

squid with spinach

KALAMARAKIA ME HORTA

1 kg fresh squid or cuttlefish

4–5 tablespoons extra virgin olive oil

1 large onion, sliced

2 garlic cloves, crushed

5 tablespoons white wine

150 ml hot water

750 g fresh spinach, trimmed, rinsed and drained

a small bunch of dill, coarsely chopped

sea salt and freshly ground black pepper

SERVES 6

Clean the squid by pulling the head away from the body. Slice the bodies open and discard all the innards, including the elongated transparent quill. Pull the skin off the bodies and discard, but keep the 2 small fins on the sides. Slice each head across horizontally just under the eyes and keep the tentacles, discarding the head and the round beak in the centre. Rinse carefully, particularly the tentacles, and drain.

Cut the bodies in half vertically, then cut each piece crossways into 3 cm strips. Cut the tentacles into 2–3 smaller pieces.

Heat the oil in a large saucepan, add the onion and sauté until translucent. Increase the heat, add the squid and garlic and keep stirring until all the moisture it produces has evaporated and it starts to turn golden, about 10–15 minutes.

Add the wine and let it bubble gently for a few minutes. Add the water, salt and pepper, cover and cook for 30 minutes, stirring occasionally to prevent sticking.

Pat the spinach dry in a clean tea towel, chop coarsely and add to the squid, stirring well. Cover and cook for 15 more minutes. Stir in the dill and serve.

Mussels appear in some of the signature dishes of Thessaloniki. You will find this version in small *mezethopolia* (meze restaurants) in the Modiano Market or on pavement tables in Lathathika, the old area of the city. Mussels are farmed in the bay and you can see them spreading out over the glass-like sea. They are sparkling fresh, but the great advantage is that you can buy them in the markets already shelled, sold in clear plastic bags with some of their liquid. No scrubbing and cleaning. Bliss!

fresh mussels with saffron and lemon

MIDIA SAGANAKI ME ZAFORA

1.5 kg live mussels, soaked in cold water

5 tablespoons dry white wine

4–5 tablespoons extra virgin olive oil

1 onion, finely chopped

1 garlic clove, chopped

1 green pepper, deseeded and chopped

freshly squeezed juice of ½ lemon

½ teaspoon Dijon mustard

a generous pinch of saffron, steeped in a little hot water

2 tablespoons finely chopped fresh flat leaf parsley

freshly ground black pepper

SERVES 4–6

Scrub the mussels well, knock off any barnacles and pull off the beards. Discard any broken mussels and any that won't close when they are tapped on the work surface. Rinse and drain in a colander.

Transfer to a large saucepan, add the wine and an equal amount of water, cover and cook over medium heat for 6–7 minutes, shaking the pan occasionally until they have opened. Remove with a slotted spoon into a colander resting in a bowl to catch their juices. If any remain shut at this stage, discard them too. Put the mussels on a plate and cover with clingfilm. Add any saved liquid to the saucepan and let it settle.

Heat the olive oil in a sauté or frying pan, add the onion and sauté until translucent. Add the garlic and pepper and cook for 3–4 minutes more. Add as much of the liquid from the mussels as you can, tilting the saucepan carefully in order to avoid any sediment. Alternatively, you can strain it through muslin.

Add the lemon juice, mustard and saffron liquid and boil gently for 15 minutes to reduce it. Add the mussels and a generous sprinkling of black pepper, simmer for 5 more minutes, sprinkle with parsley and serve hot.

Grilled fish is an integral part of Greek summer life and there is nothing more exhilarating than the aroma of barbecuing fish in the open air. Whenever the fishing boats bring in a large, glistening specimen, such as tuna or swordfish, it is inevitably made into souvlakia by the restaurants that evening. The kebabs could be served with Tzatziki (page 16) or Tarator (page 16), and a substantial salad like Horiatiki Salata (page 19).

600 g thick tuna steaks, cut into 5 cm cubes

2–3 small red onions, quartered

2–3 mixed coloured peppers, deseeded and sliced into 8 pieces each

5–6 sprigs of parsley, to serve

MARINADE

3 tablespoons olive oil

freshly squeezed juice of 1 large lemon

2 garlic cloves, crushed

1 green chilli, deseeded and finely chopped

1 tablespoon dried oregano, such as Greek rigani

1 teaspoon dried thyme

a handful of fresh parsley, finely chopped

sea salt and freshly ground black pepper

6 metal skewers

MAKES 6

grilled tuna kebabs
TONOS SOUVLAKI

To make the marinade, put the olive oil, lemon juice, garlic, chilli, oregano, thyme, parsley, salt and pepper in a large bowl and beat well. Add the tuna pieces and stir to coat. Cover with clingfilm and chill in the refrigerator for 2–3 hours, stirring occasionally.

Separate the onion quarters into 2–3 pieces each, according to their size. Remove the tuna cubes from the marinade. Starting with a piece of pepper, thread pieces of tuna, onion and pepper onto a skewer, finishing with a piece of pepper. Repeat with the remaining skewers.

Barbecue over hot coals for 5–7 minutes on each side according to the strength of the fire, basting with the leftover marinade as they cook. Alternatively, cook under a preheated grill on all sides, about 10 cm from the heat, for 6–8 minutes in total. Take care as tuna can become dry if overcooked.

Meanwhile, put the remaining marinade into a small saucepan and boil for 2–3 minutes. To serve, arrange the skewers on a platter with sprigs of parsley and drizzle some of the leftover marinade juices over the top.

Long metal skewers of glistening grilled chicken or lamb, with enticing garlicky aromas, were one of the culinary delights of old Beirut. A proper charcoal or wood fire is infinitely more enticing than an indoor grill, but use whatever is convenient. Serve hot with Tarator (page 16) or Tzatziki (page 16), and salads, such as the Lebanese classic, Tabbouleh (page 20) – its fresh herby aromas fuse deliciously with the spicy flavours of the kebabs.

750 g boneless chicken, cut into large cubes

2 small red onions, quartered

2 red or yellow peppers, deseeded and sliced into 8 pieces each

MARINADE

4 tablespoons olive oil

freshly squeezed juice of 1 lemon

3 garlic cloves, crushed

1 teaspoon ground cumin

½ teaspoon ground allspice

½ teaspoon ground sumac*

sea salt and freshly ground black pepper

TO SERVE

6 small pita breads

2 tablespoons fresh parsley, chopped

6 metal skewers

MAKES 6

spicy chicken kebabs

DAJAJ MESHWI

To make the marinade, put all the ingredients in a large bow and whisk well. Add the chicken cubes and turn to coat well. Cover and chill in the refrigerator for 6 hours or overnight.

Pull the onion quarters into layers of 2 or 3. Starting with a piece of chicken, thread pieces of chicken, onion and pepper onto a skewer, then repeat with the remaining skewers. Barbecue over hot coals for 8–10 minutes on each side until golden, turning frequently. Alternatively, cook under a preheated grill, about 10 cm from the heat, for 12–15 minutes, turning frequently.

Split the pita breads along one side and heat them on the barbecue or under the grill. Invite people to make their own kebabs by filling the pita with grilled chicken, peppers, parsley and onions. Alternatively, lay the hot pitas on a platter, pull the chicken and vegetables off the skewers and scatter on top. Sprinkle with parsley and serve immediately.

Note Ground sumac is available from Middle Eastern stores.

Variation Lamb Kebabs (*Lahem Meshwi*)

Add 1 teaspoon ground coriander and 3 tablespoons plain yoghurt to the marinade, but omit the sumac. Instead of chicken, use 1 kg boneless lamb (preferably leg meat), cut into 4 cm cubes. Thread the meat onto the skewers and barbecue for 20–30 minutes, turning frequently, or grill for 10–12 minutes. Pull the meat off the skewers and serve on a large platter, sprinkled with thinly sliced red onion and 1 tablespoon sumac, with hot pita breads.

STUFFING

3 tablespoons olive oil

2 large onions, finely chopped

600 g minced lamb

1 teaspoon ground allspice

1 teaspoon ground cinnamon

2 tablespoons pomegranate syrup
or 2 tablespoons freshly squeezed
lemon juice

150 ml hot water

3–4 tablespoons pine nuts,
toasted in a dry frying pan

4 tablespoons chopped
fresh parsley

sea salt and freshly
ground black pepper

KIBBEH

225 g fine bulghur

1 large onion

500 g finely minced beef or lamb

1 teaspoon ground allspice

1 teaspoon ground cinnamon

100 g butter

sea salt and freshly
ground black pepper

TO SERVE

Tzatziki (page 16)

a selection of salads

*a roasting tin, 30 x 24 x 5 cm,
generously buttered on the
bottom and sides with 50 g butter*

MAKES 12 PIECES

Kibbeh has an almost mythical status in Lebanese cooking. Before food processors appeared, it involved a lot of manual pounding, so it was mostly made for special occasions – not so now.

baked kibbeh

KIBBEH BIL-SANIYEH

To make the stuffing, heat the oil in a saucepan, add the onions and sauté until they start to turn golden. Increase the heat, add the meat and sauté until the moisture has evaporated and it starts to sizzle, 10–12 minutes. Add the allspice and cinnamon and fry for 2–3 minutes. Add salt, pepper, the pomegranate syrup and water, cover and simmer for 30 minutes. Remove from the heat and stir in the pine nuts and chopped parsley.

To make the kibbeh, soak the bulghur in a bowl of cold water for 10 minutes. Change the water once and soak for another 5 minutes. Drain.

Put the onion in a food processor and pulse until finely chopped. Add the minced lamb, allspice, cinnamon, salt and pepper. Process until smooth. Transfer to a bowl and add the drained bulghur. Have a bowl of cold water with some ice cubes in it ready. Wet your hand in the cold water and knead the mixture for a few minutes. Divide the kibbeh mixture into 2 portions.

Dip your hands in the cold water, take a small handful from one of the kibbeh portions, flatten it between your palms and spread it neatly at the base of the roasting tin. Continue, wetting your hands and joining the pieces neatly and overlapping slightly until the whole base is covered to about 1 cm thick.

Spread the stuffing evenly over the base. Use the remaining kibbeh mixture to cover the top in the same way as before, by stretching and patching like a patchwork quilt. Lebanese cooks decorate the top with intricate patterns before baking, but I think it is enough to score it with a sharp knife into diamond, rectangular or square serving portions.

Dot the butter over the top and bake in a preheated oven at 180°C (350°F) Gas 4 for 20–30 minutes. (Do not overcook or it will become very dry.) Run a sharp knife around the edges, then cut the pieces carefully and lift individually onto a platter. Serve hot or at room temperature with Tzatziki and salads.

1 large onion

700 g minced beef or
a mixture of minced lamb
and minced beef

2 garlic cloves, crushed

1 egg, lightly beaten

1 teaspoon ground cumin

½ teaspoon ground allspice

a pinch of ground cinnamon

3 tablespoons finely chopped
fresh coriander

3 tablespoons olive or
groundnut oil

sea salt and freshly
ground black pepper

THE SAUCE

6 tablespoons olive or
groundnut oil

1 large onion, finely chopped

1 teaspoon plain flour

½ teaspoon ground allspice

½ teaspoon ground coriander

2 tablespoons pomegranate
syrup or freshly squeezed
juice of ½ lemon

200 ml hot water

sea salt and freshly
ground black pepper

TO SERVE

3 tablespoons pine nuts,
toasted in a dry frying pan

pita bread

MAKES ABOUT 20

Delicate meatballs with a silky texture and exotic spicy aromas are the crown of Lebanese cuisine. Ideally, the meat is minced twice to achieve this softness, but even then it is the dexterity of the women's fingers kneading it patiently which achieves these silky results. Pomegranate syrup is one of my favourite ingredients and it adds a new dimension to this dish. Its addition is inspired by a similar recipe by my friend Anissa Helou in her book *Lebanese Cuisine*.

meatballs with pine nuts

DAOUD PASHA

Put the onion in a food processor and pulse until coarsely chopped. Add the minced beef, garlic, egg, cumin, allspice, cinnamon, salt and pepper and process until smooth. Add the coriander and pulse briefly. Transfer to a bowl. Take small spoonfuls of the mixture and shape them into walnut-sized balls with your hands. Set aside.

Heat the oil in a non-stick frying pan, add the meatballs in batches and fry gently, rolling them until they brown all over.

Meanwhile, to make the sauce, heat the oil in a large saucepan, add the onion and sauté gently until translucent. Sprinkle with the flour, salt, pepper, allspice and ground coriander and stir for 2–3 minutes more. Add the pomegranate syrup and the water, cover and simmer for 10 minutes.

Add the meatballs and roll to coat them in the sauce. Cover and simmer for 10 more minutes, shaking the pan occasionally to prevent them from sticking. Sprinkle with pine nuts and serve hot with pita bread.

The delicious aroma of keftethes frying in the kitchen always brings a celebratory air with it. No social gathering in Greece is complete without them. Greek women pride themselves in shaping them into tiny, round, walnut-size balls – the smaller the better – but of course you don't have to do that. My childhood friend Maria is a wonderful cook and makes the best keftethes I know. But then she also makes the best dolmathes and the best fricassée, so it is a real treat to be invited by her when I am in Athens. Athens is my home city: it holds a lot of treats for me, but this is one of the best.

fried meatballs

KEFTETHES

3 medium slices of bread, crusts discarded and soaked in water

500 g minced beef or lamb

1 tablespoon freshly squeezed lemon juice or white wine

1 onion, grated

1 egg, lightly beaten

1 tablespoon dried oregano, such as Greek rigani

a small bunch of mint, chopped

5 tablespoons plain flour

4–5 tablespoons sunflower oil

sea salt and freshly ground black pepper

MAKES ABOUT 15

Drain the bread and squeeze out the excess water, then put the bread in a bowl. Add the minced beef, lemon juice, onion, egg, oregano, mint, salt and pepper. Mix it with your fingers until well amalgamated.

Put the flour on a work surface. Make round, walnut-sized balls of the mince mixture, then roll them lightly in the flour. For ordinary meals at home, you can make them bigger, then flatten them – this will make frying quicker.

Heat the oil in a non-stick frying pan, add the meatballs and fry, turning them around until golden on all sides. Remove and drain on kitchen paper, then serve immediately.

If there was a beauty contest for fruit, quinces would be among the strongest contenders. These golden fruit bear the prettiest of flowers and, in autumn, are found in open-air street markets, in restaurants and hanging on the bare tree-branches, sparkling and shimmering in the sun. Quinces can be roasted whole in the oven and served with whipped cream, made into preserves or added to casseroles with lamb, beef or pork.

pork with quinces

HIRINO ME KYTHONIA

3 tablespoons olive oil

6 boneless steaks of pork tenderloin, about 1 kg, or 6 leg steaks

freshly squeezed juice of 1 lemon

2–3 allspice berries (optional)

450 ml hot water

2 quinces, about 750 g

4–5 tablespoons sunflower oil

2 tablespoons demerara sugar

¼ teaspoon ground cinnamon

sea salt

SERVES 6

Heat the olive oil in a large saucepan over high heat, add the pork and fry until brown on both sides. Reduce the heat, pour half the lemon juice over the meat and let it evaporate for 2–3 minutes. Add the allspice berries, if using, and the hot water, cover and simmer for 30 minutes, adding a little salt towards the end.

Meanwhile, fill a large bowl with cold water and add the remaining lemon juice. Cut the quinces in quarters, then core and peel them. Put the quince quarters in the bowl of acidulated water straight away to stop them discolouring.

Drain the quinces and pat them dry. Slice each piece in half vertically. Heat the oil in a large frying pan. Working in batches, add as many of the quince slices as you can in one layer and fry slowly over gentle heat until golden. When they start to colour, turn each piece over and let them brown on the other side, 15–20 minutes. Spread on top of the pork.

Sprinkle with sugar and cinnamon and add a little more hot water until the quinces are almost covered. Tilt the saucepan to mix the ingredients. Cover and cook slowly for 45 minutes until tender. Do not stir after the quinces have been added, but lift and shake the saucepan gently instead. Serve hot.

index